Sociology Revision
AS-Level
Family Revision &
Test Yourself Booklet
Ideal for Resits

SOCIOLOGYTWYNHAM.COM

ISBN-13: 978-150/816820
ISBN-10: 1507816820

ACKNOWLEDGEMENT

Special thanks to pixabay.com for allowing the use of their image on the front cover.

CONTENTS

PLEASE NOTE

This test yourself booklet has been designed to test your knowledge in the multiple-choice questions and understanding in the short question section.
First and foremost this is a revision guide book designed to supplement rather than replace your text book.
The guide has also been designed to accompany this booklet so you can address and misunderstandings you might have and improve your examination performance.

1 THE FAMILY AND HOUSEHOLD REVISION

Defining the family - the Office of National statistics defines the family as: "a married, civil partnered or cohabiting couple with or without children, or a lone parent with at least one child.

Types of families - there are several types of recognized family structures; blended/reconstituted family; extended family; gay or lesbian family; lone parent family; nuclear family; modified extended family; polygamous family; beanpole family and symmetrical family.

Defining a household- at its simplest a household consists of one person living alone or a group of people who share living arrangements at the same address for example a group of university students.

COMPETING PERSPECTIVES OF THE FAMILY (in other words different views on what the family is for)

There are different or competing perspectives on the family: Functionalist; Marxist; Feminist; New Right and Postmodern.

- **Functionalist perspective**: argues the family is a functional prerequisite as it plays the key role in maintaining social stability. Murdock examined 250 societies and found the family performs four basic functions:

    1. Sexual – the family provides stable sexual relationships for adults and controls the sexual habits of its members
    2. Reproduction – helps provide new members of society
    3. Socialization – teaches children the norms and values of society to keep society functioning
    4. Economic – pools resources for all family members to share

- For Parsons (1951) the function of the family has two basic functions:

    1. primary socialization of children – see page 4
    2. stabilisation of adult personalities – see page 4

1

- **Marxist perspective:** sees the family as a tool of capitalism.

- Engles argued the nuclear family solved the problem of inheritance of private property.

- Althusser (1971) a French Marxist, argued that in order for capitalism to survive people must be taught how to think and behave, and the family is one of the best mechanisms for doing this. This is because the family is seen to help maintain the dominant position of the ruling class by teaching family members to submit to authority.

- Contemporary Marxists like Zaretsky (1976) see the family as an aid to capitalism because:

    1. the capitalist system is built on the domestic labour of housewives who produce future workers
    2. at the same time, the family consumes the products of capitalism, which perpetuates the profits for the ruling-class

- **Feminist perspectives:** view the family as oppressing women. There are three feminist approaches:

- **Radical feminists:** focus squarely on patriarchy as the instrument of oppression (emasculation) within the home. This perspective is evident in the work of Bryson (1992) who sees the oppression of women by men (patriarchy) as universal. Delphy and Leonard (1992) argue it is men rather than capitalism who benefit the most from exploiting women and the family is central in maintaining this structure as:

    1. families are structured; in this structure men dominate while women and children are subordinate (very few families are matriarchal)
    2. man's position in the family is the dominant one he tends to make the final decision on family issues
    3. while women have paid employment outside the home, yet they still have to undertake household tasks – this is known as the dual burden
    4. while some women have paid employment outside the home yet still remain responsible for the majority of household tasks and care for children – this is known as the triple-shift

- **Marxist feminists:** argue women's oppression benefits capitalism. Benston (1972) argues capitalism benefits from a large army of women – an unpaid workforce - who are compliant and willing to do as they're told because women have been socialized to act this way and women rears future workers to think the same way.

- Both radical and Marxist feminists argue the abolition of the family is needed to end women's oppression.

- **Liberal feminists':** argue is women's oppression can be overcome by:

    1. changing the socialization patterns of males and females
    2. improving legislation on equal pay; divorce etc.

- **New Right perspective:** very similar in principle to functionalists - are concerned about the decline of the nuclear family.

    1. John Redwood (1993) a Conservative MP argued the natural state is for two parents to look after their children. The breadwinner husband and homemaker-wife model is the best structure for self-reliance, reducing the likelihood of welfare dependency

    2. Easier access to divorce has increased the number of single parents who are too dependent on welfare for their livelihood

    3. Charles Murray argues a welfare dependency has created a dependency culture as individuals find welfare benefits far more tempting than finding work. Murray termed the work-shy as the underclass

    4. New Right argue social policies have helped increase family diversity in the form of reconstituted and lone parent families have undermined the traditional family

- **Postmodernist perspective:** position focuses on there no longer being a perfect type of family structure as families are fashioned a refashioned to meet changing social and cultural needs – think of same sex families.

    1. Postmodernists see family diversity as an expression of personal choice and lifestyle choice (a point which makes the New Right shudder)

    2. Judith Stacey (1990) argues the diversity of family types has established themselves to the extent there will never be one dominant type in Western society again

CHANGING FAMILY STRUCTURES OVER TIME

- Pre-Industrial Families (pre-industrial means before industrialization) had large numbers of children. Family life in the pre-industrial period was characterized by the dominance of a family-based economy where work is mostly agricultural.

- Classic extended family in pre-industrial society, kinship dominates and the multifunctional extended family is the normal family structure. This structure consisted of male head of the family, his wife and children and aging parents. This type of family structure was common in the pre-industrial period:

  1. together the family worked as a productive unit producing the things needed to sustain the family's survival

  2. kin relationship during this period is one of binding obligations where an individual's status was ascribed

  3. during the industrialization period the function (purpose) of the family was multifunctional: economic production; educational; political; *ascribed status*

- Industrialization (the period from the start of the industrial revolution) functionalists say industrialization changed the function of the family. Parsons argues the nuclear family best meets the needs of industrial society as it allows individuals to achieve status. In addition *Parsons* argues the family now had two essential functions to perform because the nuclear family becoming structurally isolated – the isolated nuclear family:

  1. primary socialization – children learning society's culture helping establish a value consensus
  2. stabilization of adult personalities via the sexual division of labour (instrumental & expressive roles)

The above was due to the isolated nuclear family being:

  1. free from binding obligations to wider kin
  2. able to be geographically and socially mobile

The above points show how the nuclear family fits with the needs of industrial society by being structured to move to where work is and by rewarding individual achievement – *achieved status.* Therefore Parsons is arguing industrialization changed the roles and status of individuals within the family.

This social change means institutions become specialized – structural differentiation. Structural differentiation meant the state via the National Health Service (NHS); compulsory education and welfare services took on many of the traditional functions of the family, leaving the family to specialize in its two essential functions of primary socialization and the stabilization of adult personalities.

Parsons 'then and now' approach to family change was brought into question by research based evidence from other sociologists: Willmott and Young; Laslett; Anderson; Oakley argue there was more variety in family forms than Parsons suggests, see below:

Name	How has industrialization changed the family?
Talcott Parsons	The isolated nuclear family: 1. Led to the isolation of the nuclear family away from their wider kin 2. Loss of traditional functions undertaken by classic extended family 3. Status now achieved (was ascribed) 4. Has become a mobile workforce
Peter Laslett	1. Found only 10% of households between 1564-1821 included kin (fitted classic extended model) 2. Laslett argues nuclear families were the norm in pre-industrial England
Michael Anderson	1. Argues the early stages of industrialization encouraged extended families 2. Anderson took a sample of homes in Preston and found the working class relied on families for support 3. Overcrowding was an issue as people shared homes to save rent
Women in Families – Ann Oakley	1. 1842 Mines Act – banned women from being miners 2. Around same time laws were passed preventing women being employed in industries 3. Above caused economic dependence of women on men 4. Above meant the isolation of housework and child care from being seen as 'work' 5. Women 'forced' to adopt mother/housewife as primary role
Willmott and Young Symmetrical family	Identify four stages in the development of the family: 1. Stage 1 (up to 1750) the pre - industrial family was a unit of economic production with the main family structure being nuclear 2. Stage 2 (from 1750 to 1900) most working class families in industrial areas were extended families with an growing difference between work in the home and paid employment 3. Stage 3 (from 1900) symmetrical family becomes the norm, with more family life centred around the home – *hence privatised nuclear family* - with: • free time being devoted to chores and odd-jobs • leisure is mainly home-based with increased TV usage • strong conjugal bonds • husband and wife relationships more about companionship by sharing experiences in and outside the home 4. Stage 4 (the future) they predicted a family structure characterised by 'work-centred' individuals

Demographic trends also influence family structures

Other influences on family size are changing birth rates; increased life expectancy and improved infant mortality rates. These changes are largely due to:

1. advances in medicine, public hygiene and health education
2. welfare state (social security)
3. nutrition and diet
4. working conditions
5. rise of individualism

Social policies also influence family structures

Social policy refers to government legislation (laws on abortion; marriage; divorce etc) and activities (policies which shape education; health; taxation etc) which seek to improve the wellbeing of its people (as discussed above, social policies on childhood). Therefore politicians use legislation to influence family structures.

In 1945 The Welfare State was a social policy set up to allow the state to support families through:

* welfare benefits, housing, health-care and education

During 1960s and 1970s legislation helped influence family structure:

* the 1969 Divorce Reform Act made it easier for women to file for divorce which was seen to threaten the family by some politicians as it increased the number of families headed by women (a point which did not trouble feminists)

From 1979 the Conservative Government wanted to protect traditional family with

* Child Support Agency (CSA) – kept tabs on 'errant fathers'

* Children Act 1989 – gave children rights

From 1997 the New Labour Government recognized family diversity as well as marriage

* 'Supporting Families' consultation paper valued marriage for families

* yet their 2005 civil partnership legislation recognized the diversity of family structures

From 2010 the Conservative Government still values traditional family structures through:

* welfare policies which reduce individuals' dependency on the state (cutting benefit payments) and increases it on the family by making the family take care of the individuals within it such as an unemployed spouse by pooling resources instead of claiming welfare

Feminists argue the Conservatives and the New Right social policies seek to keep women in the home while New

Labour might recognize family diversity but still support patriarchal society through social policies which keep women as primary carer.

An assessment of social policies from the competing perspectives:

New Right thinkers (popular with the Conservative Party) argue social policies should be designed to support the nuclear family. As the nuclear family is constructed on breadwinner/homemaker model, social policies need to encourage self-reliance which would reduce a culture of dependence identified by Charles Murray as being a cause of many social ills. Criticisms – feminists would point out it tries to force women back into subordinate role. It also assumes patriarchal nuclear family is 'natural' rather than socially constructed. Marxists would point out it would push more working-class families into poverty.

Marxists point out how social policies serve the ruling class at the expense of the working class. Althusser (1971) argued that in order for capitalism to survive people must be taught how to think and behave, and the family is one of the best mechanisms for doing this as it gets working-class parents to put their children through an education system which produces obedient and docile workers. Another example is the low level of state pension for workers too old to work are being 'sustained' at lowest possible cost.

However functionalists point out the purpose of social policies is the way they function/contribution they make towards social stability. Functionalists like Fletcher see social policy as an outcome of the march of progress towards a society where the family is assisted by the state rather than social policies being a form of state social control. Criticisms – feminists would point out it assumes all members of the family benefit from social policies. Marxists would point out it assumes there is a march of progress for everyone.

Feminists argue social policies are still constructed on the belief women and children are dependent on a male breadwinner and so the function (purpose) of social polices is to keep society patriarchal. For example women's maternity leave is much longer than men's paternity leave, the assumption being women will automatically look after the children. Criticisms - Not all policies put women in second place. Equal Pay laws; welfare - benefits for lone parents and equal right to divorce can be seen to challenge patriarchy.

Jacques Donzelot (1997) argues the state uses social policies to regulate people's behaviour by using doctors and social workers to control and change behaviour within families. This process is not equally targeted between classes as poor families are seen as more likely to be a 'problem' in need of 'improvement.' Rachel Condry (2007) study 'Families Shamed', examined the relationship between the state and the family, and its expectations about family responsibilities.

CHANGING FAMILY STRUCTURES (family diversity)

Changing social attitudes have created an increasing diversity of family structures. The number of nuclear families as a proportion of all households has decreased challenging the media's obsession with the cereal packet family (*Edmund Leech*, 1968) as the norm. An increasing number of households are now reconstituted/blended/step-families; same sex families or single-person households highlighting the diversity of family forms in the UK, a point which contradicts the media's continued use of the 'cereal packet family' image in for example advertising.

Characteristics of family diversity identified by *Rapoport and Rapoport* (1982) are:

1. organisational diversity - different patterns of work outside and inside the home, and to changing marital trends resulting in a greater democratisation of domestic labour
2. cultural diversity - from indigenous to migrant households from diverse regions such as Western Europe; Middle Eastern; Southeast Asia etc. bring their own unique family and household composition. Afro-Caribbean households are more likely to be single-parent families while South Asian families are traditionally extended families but increasingly they are favouring more nuclear family households than in the past.
3. social class diversity - is demonstrated through joint conjugal roles in middle-class couples; segregated conjugal roles in working-class families. Middle-classes have a higher proportion of nuclear families compared to inner-city working-classes who have a higher proportion of lone-parent households. In addition extended families are still found in traditional working-class areas of the UK
4. family life course diversity - different stages of family structure during key periods, e.g. newlywed couples; couples having children; retired couples
5. life cycle diversity - which exists between families whose members are from different generations e.g. grandparents having different attitudes to cohabitation and divorce

The above helps explain the reasons for the diversity of family structures away from the traditional nuclear family structure identified by Murdock and Parsons (functionalists).

There are two main ways of explaining the growth in family diversity. As mentioned above, functionalists see the nuclear family as the 'correct' family structure, a point exemplified in Leach's cereal packet family. The New Right are in agreement with functionalists as they too identify the nuclear family as being the 'correct' structure. From this any family diversity away from the nuclear family 'norm' is dysfunctional (the opposite of functional).

In contrast, radical feminism and postmodern perspectives do not see the nuclear family as being the ideal family structure. From these two perspectives any set of relationships can be defined as a family by those people involved.

Giddens identifies these changes to family and marriage as part of the transformation of intimacy. Couples now build their relationships on the quality of their relationships rather than the more traditional obligations of economic dependence or a sense of loyalty. Giddens used the term confluent love to describe what keeps couples together in the modern world.

Changing family structures (diversity) due to the influence of marriage, cohabitation, childbearing, divorce etc.

Marriage Timeline

- 1753 – Clandestine Marriage Act: First time the state regulated marriage
- 1836 – Marriage Act introduces Civil marriages: Marriage becomes a civil institution as well as a religious one
- 1949 – Marriage Act: The main piece of legislation regarding marriage
- 2004 – Civil Partnership Act: The first legally recognized relationship for same-sex couples
- 2013 July: Marriage (Same Sex Couples) Act becomes law, making equal marriage legal
- 2014 by Summer: First same sex weddings to take place

Marriage

- marriage remains popular with most adults being married or re-marrying after divorce
- In 2013 there were 18.2 million families in the UK. Of these, 12.3 million consisted of a married couple with or without children
- since the 1970s the amount of marriages has decreased from 480,000 in 1972 to 283,000 in 2005
- over the past 40 years people tend to get married later (could be due to popularity of cohabitation)
- the number of first marriages has fallen but remarriages have increased especially after the Divorce Reform Act of 1969 and then levelled off

Reasons for decrease in marriage over past 40 years:

- secularization
- people wary of marriage
- acceptance of cohabitation
- women's rights – focus on career and not being a housewife (Sue Sharpe studied working-class girls in 1970 and found concerns were marriage, children etc. In 1990 she found girls' priorities had changed to their career and independence)

Cohabitation – their temporary nature could be contributing towards an increase in lone-parent family structures

Over the past 40 years cohabitation has grown significantly in popularity. The number of opposite sex cohabiting couple families has increased significantly, from 2.2 million in 2003 to 2.9 million in 2013. Eleanor Macklin (1975) identifies four types of motivations for cohabitation:

- temporary casual for convenience
- affectionate dating
- trial marriage
- temporary alternative to marriage
- permanent alternative to marriage

Childbearing – birth rates affect family size e.g. 100 years' ago families had more children, consequently were larger

The growth in cohabitation as helped remove the stigma of births outside marriage to the extent that the number of births outside marriage has increased to around 50% of all births in 2013. At the same time women are having fewer children or having them later in life (2013 average age of becoming a mother increased to 30 years) or indeed remaining childless. Beck (1992) suggests this latter change is due to the increasing contradiction between women's domestic roles and paid employment. But it could also be due to the rising cost of childcare.

Ethnicity also determines the birth rate, and the age that women have children. Overall, Bangladeshi and Pakistani women are the most fertile and the extent of the gap between Indian and Bangladeshi women illustrates the importance of distinguishing between specific ethnic minority groups, rather than treating all Asians as a single category. In most of the ethnic groupings, the birth rate peaked at age 25-29, although for Pakistani women, the peak is at the earlier age of 20-24.

Divorce – an increase in divorce rates could be contributing to more blended and lone-parent families as well as a rise in singlehood in the over 45s

The number of divorces in the UK have risen sharply since the 1970s with around 42% of all marriages ending in divorce. There are several reasons for this increase:

- Legal changes – the 1969 Divorce Reform Act made it easier for women to file for divorce
- Changes in women's position – equal job opportunities meant women were less dependent on their husbands
- Secularisation – declining influence of religion
- Ease – divorce has become easier to obtain
- Stigma – less stigma (socially acceptable) attached to divorce. According to Cockett and Tripp normalisation of divorce has occurred making it easier to deal with a failed marriage
- Higher expectations – couples have higher expectations from their marriage. Allan and Crow found individuals seek fulfilment and divorce if it's not found
- Rise of individualism – Beck (2001) said society today is individualised, and as a result self-expression and independence can put a strain on a marriage

Who divorces?

- age – the younger you get married the more likely to divorce due to money issues; growing apart
- old age – the number of people aged 60+ is increasing due to increased life expectancy; loss of stigma and ever increasing economic freedom for women
- social class – the lower the class position of the breadwinner, the more likely to divorce due to financial problems
- parents – the offspring of divorced parents are more likely to divorce themselves
- region - In 2014 Wales had the highest proportion of divorced adults (9.7%) with Northern Ireland the lowest (5.5%). England (9%) Scotland (8.2%)

However, divorce also adds additional pressures on marriage. But at the same time it's important to recognize marriages do 'end' without couples resorting to formal legal proceedings as they:

1. Separate – separation is where couples effectively end their marriage, but remain legally together and still live under the same roof

2. Empty-shell marriage – where a couple remains legally married but love, sex and companionship are in the past

The effects of the rising divorce rates are open to competing interpretations. For the New Right rising divorce rates are an outcome of permissiveness eroding the family, along with family values. While functionalists are concerned about the decline of the nuclear family caused by increasing family diversity. They see rising divorce rates as evidence of higher expectations between couples resulting in less dysfunctional families. Therefore divorce can be seen to have a positive function.

Marxist feminists' argue rising divorce rates are an outcome of the tensions caused by the dual-burden of capitalism. At home women are forced to undertake unpaid labour, while in the workplace they tend to occupy jobs with low wages. Radical feminists would point out increasing divorce rates are an outcome of the dark-side of family life being more openly discussed allowing women to leave oppressive relationships as well as protecting children from witnessing violent relationships.

Rodgers and Pryor (1998) reviewed 200 studies attempting to find out if divorce had a negative effect on children. Children of separated families have a higher probability of:

- being in poverty and poor housing;
- being poorer when they are adults;
- behavioural problems;
- performing less well in school;
- leaving school/home when young;
- becoming sexually active, pregnant, or a parent at an early age;
- depressive symptoms, high levels of smoking and drinking, and drug use during adolescence and adulthood.

Rodgers and Pryor suggested divorce alone does not cause the above problems but occurred in association with other factors which affected the outcomes when divorce occurred.

Factors affecting outcomes of divorce:

- financial hardship can limit educational achievement;
- family conflict before, during and after separation can contribute to behavioural problems;
- parental ability to recover from distress of separation affects children's ability to adjust
- multiple changes in family structure increase the probability of poor outcomes;
- quality contact with the non-resident parent can improve outcomes.

In contrast Jon Bernardes (1997) studies concluded divorce may be less damaging to children than living with parents in constant conflict.

Whichever argument is seen as the stronger sociologists are interested in the way divorce and remarriage is helping to increase the trend towards family diversity and within this diversity new relationships are emerging. Many families are reconstituted/blended after divorce and as Carol Smart (2001), co-author of 'The Changing Experience of Childhood' found:

- there is no 'hand-book' on how to be a good step-parent as "a new etiquette is still emerging"

Singlehood

The composition of singlehood shows 2.5m people between 45 and 64 living in their own home alone with the number of men living on their own increasing far more than women. So what is driving this growth? American sociologist Eric Kinenberg research identified the following points:

1. more people live alone than ever before because they can afford to and so choose to

2. social media revolution has allowed people to experience the pleasures of social life even when they're living alone

3. growth of individualism

4. young solitaires actively reframe living alone as a mark of distinction and success

Dark-side of the Family

The term 'dark side' refers to abuse within the family, particularly towards women and children. ChildLine, (the confidential helpline for children), statistics indicate the extent to which abuse is conducted by parents. The abuse comes in many forms

- Physical abuse
- Sexual abuse
- Emotional abuse
- Economic deprivation
- Threats of violence

FAMILY DYNAMICS: ROLES AND REALTIONSHIPS WITHIN THE FAMILY

Couples

Elizabeth Bott's (1957) 'Family and Social Network' looks at two contrasting types of conjugal roles: segregated and joint. Segregated conjugal roles involve a clear differentiation between the tasks undertaken by men and women, with each pursuing clearly defined and distinct activities. Joint conjugal roles – where husband and wife share tasks – encourages equal relationships where the differentiation – or 'division of labour' – is much less clear.

- Young and Willmott's (1973) 'The Symmetrical Family' detects a shift in conjugal roles which they see as reflecting a new type of relationship between younger married couples. They detect a growing trend away from traditional segregated roles towards more joint – (symmetrical) forms of relationships. The trend originated with middle class families, but increasingly they envisage, working class families adopting similar arrangements.

- Ann Oakley's (1974) 'The Sociology of Housework' underlines the persisting inequalities in family life. It was the first influential study to consider housework as 'domestic labour' (another form of employment). Her respondents depict their domestic obligations as repetitive, unfulfilling and under-appreciated. She found little to support Young and Willmott's view of family roles being 'symmetrical', with power more equally shared between couples.

- Heidi Hartmann's (1981) found that women who had jobs outside the home remained responsible for the bulk of the housework. Husbands with working wives did not tend to do any more housework than those whose wives did not. Though Hartmann appreciates the growth of working women has given them independence this freedom is often hampered by low-paid work so they are still susceptible to male dominance (patriarchy) both in the home and in wider society.

- The dual-burden coined from Arlie Hochschild's 1989 book, 'The Second Shift' describes the responsibility women have for undertaking their domestic duties on top of their paid employment. Hochschild research studied the "leisure gap" between men and women lives caused by the responsibility for looking after the home and the people living in it.

- Duncombe and Marsden's (1995) research reinforces previous studies revealing inequalities in power and domestic responsibilities. Their female respondents complained that their husbands were indifferent to their role in holding the relationship together and the 'emotional investment' they make. The upshot of this, according to the authors, is that women are frequently saddled with a 'triple shift' of obligations: outside work, housework – and emotional work.

- Delphy and Leonard (1992) recognize men do housework, but it is rather limited. Women make the largest contribution to family life, while men contribute the least but gain the most - women carry out housework and caring roles within the family as well as supporting men in their leisure and work activities. Women also help men emotionally in the home by providing 'trouble free sex' as they argue 'men best unwind post-coitally' while in return men make very little contributions to their spouse's well-being.

Covert and overt power between couples

1. overt power is power you can see such as physical abuse

2. covert power is power which is more difficult for the victim to see as controlling such as the man deciding how much housekeeping his wife should have

- Economic dependency - married women become economically dependent on their husbands especially as once children arrive women give up work in order to look after the children and even when mothers do return to work it is usually part-time rather than full-time employment. This dependency means it is much easier for men to set the agenda over important family decisions.

- Male domination (patriarchal power) - feminists see the family as male dominated as men are the bread-winners and tend to make all the key financial decisions.

- Dobash and Dobash (1995) found that most domestic violence occurs within marriage. They argue, this is due to the institution of marriage giving power to men through their wives dependency on them. Feminists have stressed the significant amount of domestic violence used by men to their own way in the family.

- Edgell (1980) found the important family decisions such as financial issues, tended to be made by the husband, while wives were free to make the trivial decisions on their own such as what 'the evening meal which consists of' or where 'they do the weekly shopping'.

- Jan Phal (1993) research found men tended to control and manage a couple's money.

CHILDREN AND CHILDHOOD

Childhood as an age status is not fixed or universal. The experience and meaning of childhood differs across societies, time periods and between different groups. This means having a childhood is not a natural or inevitable period in a person's life but a socially constructed episode.

This is because historical and cross-cultural studies have shown being a child means different things in different societies. Even in those countries where childhood does exist the period of a person's childhood is age dependent. For example in the UK laws define what a child can or cannot do, for example when a child is compelled to attend to school or is allowed to work.

- childhood experience in pre-industrial society – Aries (1960) 'Centuries of Childhood' argued in the 17th Century childhood did not exist as children were viewed as 'tiny adults' – no real difference between children and adults, from a young age and were viewed as economic assets
- early industrial period and childhood – working-class children worked alongside adults particularly in the factories, mines and mills
- later industrial period and childhood - mid 19th century Factory/Mine Acts (social policies) meant children were no longer able to work, children no longer economic assets and 1870 Education Act – children need to be supported
- 20th century onwards - children are viewed **differently to adults** in need of support and protection, children are put first, helping to create the period known as childhood: toys, clothes, TV programmes, food etc.
- social policy cementing the development of childhood through the age of consent; Factory Acts - Contemporary employment legislation; 1870 Education Act; 1980 Child care Act; 1991 Child Support Act

Neil Postman (1982) states that childhood is disappearing as the 19th century divisions between adults and children are disappearing. Children are able to experience things that previously were only available to adults. Postman argues it is the "Frankenstein Syndrome" effect of the mass media, is largely responsible for this, particularly TV, Internet and social media.

Other sociologists argue there's been an increase in child-centredness in the UK due to families being smaller; increasing affluence along with parents driving their children around more.

However Diana Gittins (1997) argues studies which treat children as one homogenized group fails to recognize the diversity of inequality between childhood experiences such as social class, gender, ethnicity and culture. Hendrick (1997) identified the discourses of childhood as being socially constructed around the Victorian image of the natural and romantic child which possessing a natural innocence. Two later discourses of childhood proposed by Hendrick (1997) were the child as a family member and the child as a state responsibility (child of the welfare state) in need of protection and care.

1 FAMILY – MULTIPLE - CHOICE QUESTIONS

Q1 - Parsons said the family has two basic functions. These two functions are:

A – the primary socialization of children and the stabilization of children's personalities

B – the stabilization of adult personalities along with the secondary socialization of children

C – the secondary socialization of children and stabilization of children's personalities

D – the primary socialization of children and the stabilization of adult personalities

Q2 – As radical feminists Delphy and Leonard argue it is

A – women rather than capitalism who benefit the most from exploiting men and the family is central in maintaining this structure

B – men rather than capitalism who benefit the most from exploiting women and the family is central in maintaining this structure

C – men rather than Marxism who benefit the most from exploiting women and the family is central in maintaining this structure

D - men rather than functionalism who benefit the most from exploiting women and the family is central in maintaining this structure

Q3 – In addition, coming from a radical feminist perspective Delphy and Leonard also argue:

A – families are structured; in this structure women dominate while men and children are subordinate (very few families are patriarchal)

B – families are structured; in this structure men dominate while women and children are subordinate (very few families are matriarchal)

C – most families are matriarchal; in this structure women dominate while men and children are subordinate (very few families are patriarchal)

D – families are structured; in this structure men and women are subordinate to children due to the 1989 Children's Act

Q4 - Marxist feminists argue women's oppression benefits capitalism. Benston argues:

A – feminism benefits from a large army of women – an unpaid workforce - who are compliant and willing to do as they're told because women have been socialized to act this way by other women subsequently women rear future workers to think the same way.

B – via the 1989 Children Act, children benefit from a large army of women – an unpaid workforce - who are compliant and willing to do as they're told because women have been socialized to act this way

C – new right thinkers like Charles Murray benefit from a large army of women – an unpaid workforce – who are compliant and willing to do as they're told and form an underclass

D - capitalism benefits from a large army of women – an unpaid workforce - who are compliant and willing to do as they're told because women have been socialized to act this way and women rears future workers to think the same way

Q5 - Marxist and radical feminist both argue the following:

A – Marxist feminists argue the abolition of the family is needed to end women's oppression but radical feminists disagree

B – Both radical and Marxist feminists argue the family is a functional prerequisite and is needed to end women's oppression

C – Both radical and Marxist feminists argue the abolition of the family is needed to end women's oppression

D - Radical feminists argue the abolition of the family is needed to end women's oppression but Marxist feminists disagree

Q6 – New Right perspectives of the family are very similar to those of

A – Marxist feminists

B – functionalists

C – Marxist

D – Radical feminists

Q7 – "The breadwinner husband and homemaker-wife model is the best structure for self-reliance, reducing the likelihood of welfare dependency" is a statement best attributed to:

A – Benston a Marxist feminist

B - Delphy and Leonard both with radical feminist perspectives

C - John Redwood a Conservative MP with a New Right perspective

D – Zaretsky from a Marxist perspective

Q8 – When discussing pre-industrial families sociologists are referring to a time period:

A – after the industrial revolution

B – during the industrial revolution

C – during the industrial revolution, but on a Friday afternoon

D – before the industrial revolution

Q9 - During the industrialization period the function (purpose) of the family was multifunctional. These functions were:

A - economic production; educational; political and ascribed status

B - economic production; educational and political

C - economic production; educational; political; ascribed status and discipline

D – educational and political

Q10 - Parsons argues the nuclear family best meets the needs of industrial society as it allows individuals to

A – work hard

B – form a family

C – eat well

D – achieve their status

Q11 – The stabilization of adult personalities occurs via:

A – hard work

B- sexual division of labour

C – economic production

D – ascribed status

Q12 – The instrumental and expressive roles adopted by adults in a nuclear family are known collectively by functionalists as:

A – the dual burden

B – the triple shift

C – matriarchy

D - the sexual division of labour

Q13 – The importance of primary socialization for Parsons is its establishment of

A – a value consensus

B- the myth of meritocracy

C – the consumption of goods to aid capitalism

D – patriarchal power

Q14 – For Parsons the benefit of the isolated nuclear family is its capacity

A – in being free from binding obligations to wider kin as well as being geographically and socially mobile

B - in being geographically and socially mobile

C - in being free from binding obligations to wider kin

D – to impose the sexual division of labour without any intrusion from nosey relatives

Q15 – Although Parsons argues the isolated nuclear family was an outcome of industrialization, other sociologists like Laslett disagree because

A - Laslett argues nuclear families were the norm in pre-industrial England

B – Laslett argues symmetrical families were the norm during industrialization

C - Laslett argues lone parent families were the norm during industrialization

D – Laslett argues same sex families were the norm during pre-industrial England

Q16 - Social policy refers to

A – government legislation and activities which seek to undermine the wellbeing of its people

B – government legislation and activities which seek to improve the wellbeing of elderly people

C – government legislation and activities which seek to improve the wellbeing of its people

D - to government legislation and activities which seek to improve the wellbeing of just children

Q17 - In 1945 The Welfare State was a social policy set up to allow the state to support families through:

A – welfare benefits and education

B – welfare benefits, housing, the-right-to-vote, health-care and education

C – housing, the-right-to-vote, education and health-care

D – welfare benefits, housing, health-care and education

Q18 - From 1979 the Conservative Government wanted to protect traditional family by introducing a social policy which 'kept tabs on errant fathers'. The agency which was established in 1993 to collect child maintenance payments is known as:

A – Child Welfare Agency (CWA)

B – Children's Income Agency (CIA)

C – Child Support Agency (CSA)

D – Children's Cash Agency (CCA)

Q19 – Feminists' argue all governmental social policies are prejudicial against women because

A – Conservatives and the New Right social policies seek to keep women in the home while New Labour might recognize family diversity but their social policies see women as being matriarchal

B - Conservatives and the New Right social policies seek to keep women in the home while New Labour might recognize family diversity but their social policies see women as being the primary carer

C – Conservatives and the New Right social policies seek to keep women out of the home while New Labour might recognize family diversity but their social policies see women as being the primary carer

D - Conservatives and the New Right social policies seek to keep men in the home while New Labour might recognize family diversity but their social policies see men as being the primary carer

Q20 - New Right thinkers argue social policies should be designed to support the nuclear family. Feminists are critical of this way of thinking because

A – the New Right assume the matriarchal nuclear family is 'natural' rather than socially constructed

B – the New Right assume the patriarchal nuclear family is socially constructed

C – the New Right assume matriarchal nuclear family is socially constructed

D – the New Right assume the patriarchal nuclear family is 'natural' rather than socially constructed

Q21 – Giddens argues couples now build their relationships on the quality of their relationships rather than the more traditional obligations of economic dependence or a sense of loyalty. This is known as

A – confluent love

B – convergent love

C – consistent love

D – conflicted love

Q22 - The characteristics of family diversity identified by *Rapoport and Rapoport* (1982) are:

A – organizational diversity, social-class diversity, family life course diversity and life cycle diversity

B – cultural diversity, social-class diversity, family life course diversity and life cycle diversity

C – cultural diversity, organizational diversity, social-class diversity, family life course diversity and life cycle diversity

D - cultural diversity, health diversity, organizational diversity, social-class diversity, family life course diversity and life cycle diversity

Q23 Gay and lesbian households, single-person households, lone-parent families, dual-worker families and reconstituted families are all examples of

A – cereal packet families

B- family homogeneity

C – family diversity

D – the dark-side of family life

Q24 – The term cereal packet family is an image giving the impression that most people live in a 'typical family' which

A – the husband is the 'breadwinner', with a wife who stays at home in order to look after the children and do the housework. Both these parents are married to each other and neither has been married before.

B - the husband is the 'breadwinner', with a wife who stays at home in order to look after the children and do the housework. Both these parents are married to each other but one of them might have been married before.

C - the husband is the 'breadwinner', with a wife who stays at home in order to look after the children and do the housework. Both these parents are married to each other but one of them has been married before bringing their children from the previous relationship with them

D - the husband is the 'breadwinner', with a male 'wife' who stays at home in order to look after the children and do the housework. Both these parents are a same-sex married couple and neither has been married before.

Q25 - Over the past 40 years cohabitation has grown in popularity. Eleanor Macklin identifies 5 motivations for this increase in popularity:

A – affectionate dating, trial marriage, temporary alternative to marriage and permanent alternative to marriage

B – secularization, people wary of marriage, acceptance of cohabitation and women's rights

C – secularization, people wary of marriage, acceptance of cohabitation, gay rights and women's rights

D - temporary casual - for convenience, affectionate dating, trial marriage, temporary alternative to marriage and permanent alternative to marriage

Q26 - Sue Sharpe studied working-class girls in 1970 and found the girls' concerns were marriage, children etc. In 1990 she found girls' priorities had changed to their career and independence. Her findings could help explain the decline decrease in marriage over past 40 years because

A – it highlighted the growth in secularization

B – it highlighted the acceptance of cohabitation

C – it highlighted the increasing influence of women's rights – focus on career and not being a housewife

D – it highlighted the increasing influence of gay rights

Q27 - The number of births outside marriage has increased to around 50% of all births in 2013. One explanation for this decrease could be due to

A – The decrease in cohabitation as helped remove the stigma of births inside marriage

B – The growth in cohabitation as helped remove the stigma of births outside marriage

C – The growth in cohabitation as helped increase the stigma of births outside marriage

D - The decrease in cohabitation as helped remove the stigma of births outside marriage

Q28 - women are having fewer children or having them later in life (2013 average age of becoming a mother increased to 30 years) or indeed remaining childless. One explanation for this increase could be due to

A – Beck suggests this latter change is due to the decreasing contradiction between women's domestic roles and paid employment

B – Beck suggests this latter change is due to women conducting less domestic roles and more paid employment

C – Beck suggests this latter change is due to women conducting more domestic roles and less paid employment

D - Beck suggests this latter change is due to the increasing contradiction between women's domestic roles and paid employment

Q29 - The number of divorces in the UK have risen sharply since the 1970s with around 42% of all marriages ending in divorce. One explanation for this could be higher expectations of marriage. Allan and Crow explains this as meaning

A - individuals seek fulfilment from marriage and divorce if it's not found

B - individuals seek nothing particular from marriage and divorce as something to do

C - individuals seek fulfilment from marriage and divorce when fulfilled

D – individuals seek fulfilment from marriage and so divorce so they can remarry

Q30 - The number of divorces in the UK have risen sharply since the 1970s with around 42% of all marriages ending in divorce. One explanation is secularization; secularization is

A - declining influence of religion on society

B – increasing influence of religion on society

C – static influence of religion on society

D – confirmation of religion never having had any influence on society

Q31 – An empty shell marriage is

A – where a couple divorces but decide to cohabit

B- where a couple remains legally married but only sexual relations remain

C - where a couple remains legally married but love, sex and companionship are in the past

D - where a couple divorce but love, sex and companionship remain

Q32 - Marxist feminists' argue rising divorce rates are an outcome of the tensions caused by the dual-burden of capitalism. The dual-burden is

A – where women are forced to undertake unpaid labour at home, while in the workplace they tend to occupy jobs with no wages

B – where women are forced to undertake unpaid labour at home, while in the workplace they tend to occupy jobs with low wages

C – where women are forced to undertake well-paid labour at home, while in the workplace they tend to occupy jobs with low wages

D - where women are forced to undertake unpaid labour at home, while in the workplace they tend to occupy jobs with high wages

Q33 - Radical feminists would point out increasing divorce rates are an outcome of the dark-side of family life being more openly discussed allowing women to

A – remain in oppressive relationships while protecting children from witnessing violent relationships

B – remain in oppressive relationships but are free to choose whether to work or not

C – leave oppressive relationships as well as protecting children from witnessing violent relationships

D – leave oppressive relationships but return to them when the situation has calmed down

Q34 - The term 'dark side' of the family refers to

A – a family home having its electricity supply cut-off due to welfare cuts

B – every family member being unemployed and on welfare

C - abuse within the family, particularly towards women and children

D – the continuing increase in divorce rates

Q35 - Elizabeth Bott's 'Family and Social Network' looks at two contrasting types of conjugal roles: segregated and joint. Segregated and joint conjugal roles are

A – Segregated conjugal roles where husband and wife share tasks. Joint conjugal roles with little or no differentiation between the tasks

B – Segregated conjugal roles involves no clear differentiation between a husband and wife's tasks. Joint conjugal roles with huge differentiation between the tasks

C – Segregated conjugal roles involve a clear differentiation between the tasks undertaken by men and women. Joint conjugal roles where husband and wife share tasks with little or no differentiation between the tasks

D – Segregated and joint conjugal roles is another term used to describe Elizabeth Bott's concept of the sexual division of labour

Q36 - Wilmott and Young's 'The Symmetrical Family' detects a shift in conjugal roles moving away from traditional segregated roles towards more

A – asymmetrical forms of relationships

B – same sex relationships

C – segregated forms of relationships

D - symmetrical forms of relationships

Q37 - Duncombe and Marsden's research reinforces previous studies revealing inequalities in power and domestic responsibilities. They coined the term the 'triple-shift' to describe the burden placed on women. The term 'triple-shift' refers to

A – voluntary work, paid work outside the home, housework and emotional work

B – voluntary work, housework and emotional work

C – housework, trouble-free sex and paid work outside the home

D – paid work outside the home, housework and emotional work

Q38 - Married women become economically dependent on their husbands especially as once children arrive women give up work in order to look after the children. Phal's research found the consequence of this on a woman's economic position within a marriage is

A – the married couple's roles became more symmetrical

B – men tended to control and manage a couple's money

C – women tended to control and manage a couple's money as they were at home all day

D – children tended to be included more in any financial decision making

Q39 - Neil Postman argues childhood is disappearing as children are able to experience things that previously were only available to adults. What term does Postman use to describe the influence of the mass media on the erosion of childhood?

A – Dracula Syndrome

B – Horror Syndrome

C - Frankenstein Syndrome

D – Childhood Syndrome

Q40 – What do you understand by the term child-centeredness

A – where children put parents first

B – where siblings put each other first

C – where parents put their children first

D – where children put themselves first

3 FAMILY - MULTIPLE CHOICE QUESTIONS: THE ANSWERS

Q1 - Parsons said the family has two basic functions. These two functions are:

D – the primary socialization of children and the stabilization of adult personalities

Q2 – As radical feminists Delphy and Leonard argue it is

B – men rather than capitalism who benefit the most from exploiting women and the family is central in maintaining this structure

Q3 – In addition, coming from a radical feminist perspective Delphy and Leonard also argue:

B – families are structured; in this structure men dominate while women and children are subordinate (very few families are matriarchal)

Q4 - Marxist feminists argue women's oppression benefits capitalism. Benston argues:

D - capitalism benefits from a large army of women – an unpaid workforce - who are compliant and willing to do as they're told because women have been socialized to act this way and women rears future workers to think the same way

Q5 - Marxist and radical feminist both argue the following:

C – Both radical and Marxist feminists argue the abolition of the family is needed to end women's oppression

Q6 – New Right perspectives of the family are very similar to those of

B – functionalists

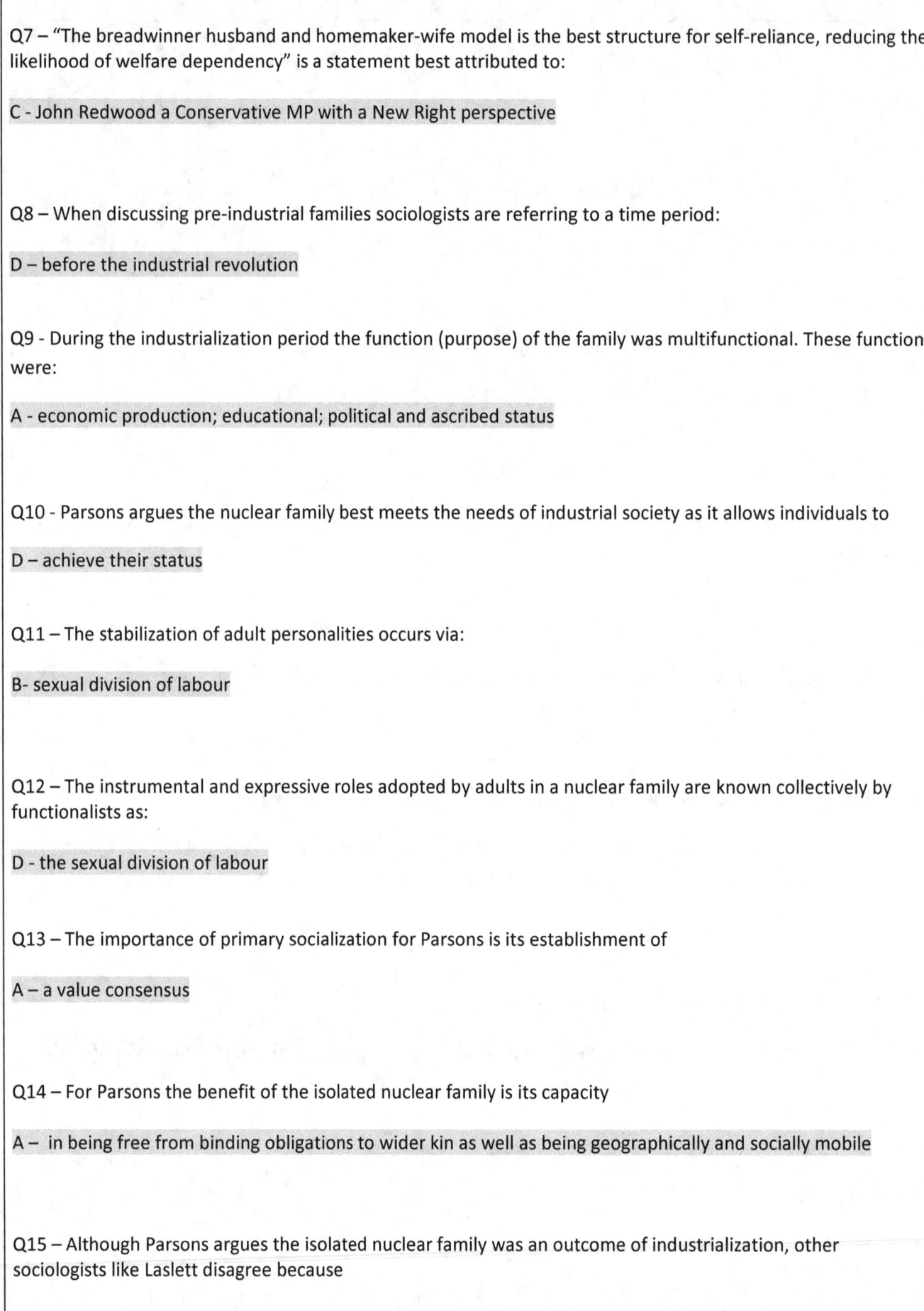

Q7 – "The breadwinner husband and homemaker-wife model is the best structure for self-reliance, reducing the likelihood of welfare dependency" is a statement best attributed to:

C - John Redwood a Conservative MP with a New Right perspective

Q8 – When discussing pre-industrial families sociologists are referring to a time period:

D – before the industrial revolution

Q9 - During the industrialization period the function (purpose) of the family was multifunctional. These functions were:

A - economic production; educational; political and ascribed status

Q10 - Parsons argues the nuclear family best meets the needs of industrial society as it allows individuals to

D – achieve their status

Q11 – The stabilization of adult personalities occurs via:

B- sexual division of labour

Q12 – The instrumental and expressive roles adopted by adults in a nuclear family are known collectively by functionalists as:

D - the sexual division of labour

Q13 – The importance of primary socialization for Parsons is its establishment of

A – a value consensus

Q14 – For Parsons the benefit of the isolated nuclear family is its capacity

A – in being free from binding obligations to wider kin as well as being geographically and socially mobile

Q15 – Although Parsons argues the isolated nuclear family was an outcome of industrialization, other sociologists like Laslett disagree because

A - Laslett argues nuclear families were the norm in pre-industrial England

Q16 - Social policy refers to

C – government legislation and activities which seek to improve the wellbeing of its people

Q17 - In 1945 The Welfare State was a social policy set up to allow the state to support families through:

D – welfare benefits, housing, health-care and education

Q18 - From 1979 the Conservative Government wanted to protect traditional family by introducing a social policy which 'kept tabs on errant fathers'. The agency which was established in 1993 to collect child maintenance payments is known as:

C – Child Support Agency (CSA)

Q19 - Feminists argue all governmental social policies are prejudicial against women because

B - Conservatives and the New Right social policies seek to keep women in the home while New Labour might recognize family diversity but their social policies see women as being the primary carer

Q20 - New Right thinkers argue social policies should be designed to support the nuclear family. Feminists are critical of this way of thinking because

D – the New Right assume the patriarchal nuclear family is 'natural' rather than socially constructed

Q21 – Giddens argues couples now build their relationships on the quality of their relationships rather than the more traditional obligations of economic dependence or a sense of loyalty. This is known as

A – confluent love

Q22 - The characteristics of family diversity identified by *Rapoport and Rapoport* (1982) are:

C – cultural diversity, organizational diversity, social-class diversity, family life course diversity and life cycle diversity

Q23 Gay and lesbian households, single-person households, lone-parent families, dual-worker families and reconstituted families are all examples of

C – family diversity

Q24 – The term cereal packet family is an image giving the impression that most people live in a 'typical family' which

A – the husband is the 'breadwinner', with a wife who stays at home in order to look after the children and do the housework. Both these parents are married to each other and neither has been married before.

Q25 - Over the past 40 years cohabitation has grown in popularity. Eleanor Macklin identifies 5 motivations for this increase in popularity:

D - temporary casual - for convenience, affectionate dating, trial marriage, temporary alternative to marriage and permanent alternative to marriage

Q26 - Sue Sharpe studied working-class girls in 1970 and found the girls' concerns were marriage, children etc. In 1990 she found girls' priorities had changed to their career and independence. Her findings could help explain the decline decrease in marriage over past 40 years because

C – it highlighted the increasing influence of women's rights – focus on career and not being a housewife

Q27 - The number of births outside marriage has increased to around 50% of all births in 2013. One explanation for this decrease could be due to

B – The growth in cohabitation as helped remove the stigma of births outside marriage

Q28 - women are having fewer children or having them later in life (in 2013 the average age of becoming a mother increased to 30 years) or indeed remaining childless. One explanation for this increase could be due to

D - Beck suggests this latter change is due to the increasing contradiction between women's domestic roles and paid employment

Q29 - The number of divorces in the UK have risen sharply since the 1970s with around 42% of all marriages ending in divorce. One explanation for this could be higher expectations of marriage. Allan and Crow explains this as meaning

A - individuals seek fulfilment from marriage and divorce if it's not found

Q30 - The number of divorces in the UK have risen sharply since the 1970s with around 42% of all marriages ending in divorce. One explanation is secularization; secularization is

A - declining influence of religion on society

Q31 – An empty shell marriage is

C - where a couple remains legally married but love, sex and companionship are in the past

Q32 - Marxist feminists' argue rising divorce rates are an outcome of the tensions caused by the dual-burden of capitalism. The dual-burden is

B – where women are forced to undertake unpaid labour at home, while in the workplace they tend to occupy jobs with low wages

Q33 - Radical feminists would point out increasing divorce rates are an outcome of the dark-side of family life being more openly discussed allowing women to

C – leave oppressive relationships as well as protecting children from witnessing violent relationships

Q34 - The term 'dark side' of the family refers to

C - abuse within the family, particularly towards women and children

Q35 - Elizabeth Bott's 'Family and Social Network' looks at two contrasting types of conjugal roles: segregated and joint. Segregated and joint conjugal roles are

C – Segregated conjugal roles involve a clear differentiation between the tasks undertaken by men and women. Joint conjugal roles where husband and wife share tasks with little or no differentiation between the tasks

Q36 - Wilmott and Young's 'The Symmetrical Family' detects a shift in conjugal roles moving away from traditional segregated roles towards more

D - symmetrical forms of relationships

Q37 - Duncombe and Marsden's research reinforces previous studies revealing inequalities in power and domestic responsibilities. They coined the term the 'triple-shift' to describe the burden placed on women. The term 'triple-shift' refers to

D – paid work outside the home, housework and emotional work

Q38 - Married women become economically dependent on their husbands especially as once children arrive women give up work in order to look after the children. Phal's research found the consequence of this on a woman's economic position within a marriage is

B – men tended to control and manage a couple's money

Q39 - Neil Postman argues childhood is disappearing as children are able to experience things that previously were only available to adults. What term does Postman use to describe the influence of the mass media on the erosion of childhood?

C - Frankenstein Syndrome

Q40 – What do you understand by the term child-centeredness

C – where parents put their children first

4 FAMILY - SINGLE QUESTIONS

Q1 Identify one reason why women today might delay having children

Q2 Identify one reason why the lives of children are seen to have improved over the past 100 years

Q3 Identify one reason why ethnic diversity over the past 50 years has increased family diversity

Q4 Identify one reason which illustrates how difference between children and adults has narrowed

Q5 Identify one reason why the number of first-time marriages are in decline

Q6 Identify one reason why women might have less children than 50 years ago

Q7 Identify one reason for increasing life expectancy

Q8 Identify two effects of women undertaking paid work on a couple's relationship

Q9 Identify two changing functions of the family

Q10 Identify two features of the symmetrical family

Q11 Identify two ways in which industrialization changed the lives of children

Q12 Identify two influences which could explain the growth in family diversity

Q13 Identify two criticisms of functionalist views of the family

Q14 Identify two criticisms of Marxist views of the family

Q15 Identify two criticisms of feminist views of the family

Q16 Identify two criticisms of radical feminist views of the family

Q17 Identify four ways in which feminist sociologists have aided our understanding of family dynamics

Q18 Identify four reasons for the for the changes in family size over the past 100 years

5 **FAMILY** – SINGLE QUESTIONS: THE ANSWERS

Q1 Identify one reason why women today might delay having children

- age at which women start having a family is rising
- women are delaying starting a family to pursue a career
- rising costs mean couples prefer to save first
- the availability of IVF and other reproductive technology 'extends' the delay
- more women are going to university and other educational opportunities

Q2 Identify one reason why the lives of children are seen to have improved over the past 100 years

- improved overall health
- improved diet and nutrition
- improved health care and associated treatments
- families more child-centred
- more rights for children
- improved education opportunities

Q3 Identify one reason why ethnic diversity over the past 50 years has increased family diversity

- more extended families
- diverse attitudes to marriage
- differing parent/child relationships
- number of children in a family
- differing attitudes to divorce
- differing relationships between husband and wife

Q4 Identify one reason which illustrates how difference between children and adults has narrowed

- children have greater access to the adult world especially via Internet
- the difference between adult and youth culture has narrowed with parents accompanying their teenage children to concerts
- aspects of social media like Facebook and Instagram are enjoyed by children and their parents for example teenagers have their parents as 'friends'
- children are increasingly economically dependent on their parents much later in life; for example children living at parental home much longer meaning the parent can still 'see' their 25 year-old offspring as a child
- lifelong learning is extending childhood for example children can now continue studying late into their twenties so the parent is still 'looking-after' their offspring

Q5 Identify one reason why the number of first-time marriages are in decline

- cohabitation has become an accepted alternative to marriage
- men are increasingly becoming fearful of divorce settlements going in a woman's favour
- some remarriages can involve people who have never married before
- less stigma associated with singlehood
- increase in divorce rates can make a couple wary of marriage

Q6 Identify one reason why women might have less children than 50 years ago

- less stigma associated with being childless
- greater career opportunities
- greater costs in bringing up children
- increased child-centredness puts a greater burden on the woman
- more availability of contraception and morning-after pill
- women defer having children to much later in life

Q7 Identify one reason for increasing life expectancy

- improved health-care facilities
- improved/better awareness of healthier diet
- improved/better awareness of health education
- improved sanitation
- improved/better awareness of available hospital treatments/medicines
- improved/better awareness of working-conditions

Q8 Identify two effects of women undertaking paid work on a couple's relationship

- gender scripts – socially constructed expectations of roles within the family could be challenged with man/husband having to do more child-care
- changing financial controls – man/husband giving up complete control
- emotional labour – child-care could become shared between husband and wife
- decision making – this could become shared between husband/wife
- divorce – added strain of wife being out at work further career could empower her to file for divorce or husband could become disgruntled and file for divorce
- expressive and instrumental roles – these could reverse with dad staying at home while wife becomes breadwinner
- dark-side of the family – wife's new role and confidence could make male partner/husband jealous and he becomes violent (domestic violence)

Q9 Identify two changing functions of the family

- social control of its members
- education
- primary and secondary socialization
- reproduction of children
- nurturing of children
- passing on property
- family was once responsible for health-care and welfare provision

Q10 Identify two features of the symmetrical family

- women in paid employment
- men helping with domestic/housework work such as washing-up
- couples sharing childcare
- couples sharing decision making
- couples sharing leisure time

Q11 Identify two ways in which industrialization changed the lives of children

- compulsory schooling/education means adult's responsibility for looking after their children is increasing
- children given rights in law as well as increasing child-centredness
- fall in infant mortality rates as well as birthrates means it's easier for a parent to focus their attention on one child than several (child-centredness)
- the mass media have turned their attention on children with dedicated programmes in addition mass media has narrowed the gap between adult and children's entertainment eg social media
- children are targeted by big business making them consumers in their own right eg pester-power

Q12 Identify two influences which could explain the growth in family diversity

- confluent love
- ageing population
- increasing divorce rates
- changing women's position
- gay rights movement
- secularization of society
- increasing trends in cohabitation
- increasing trends in singlehood
- social and legal recognition of same sex relations

Q13 Identify two criticisms of functionalist views of the family

- Murdock's views of the family are value laden, they are prejudicial against women and anti-family diversity
- ignores the dark-side of the family
- Willmott and Young – the extended family still exists which goes against the idea industrialization gave rise to the emergence of the nuclear family and it being geographically mobile

Q14 Identify two criticisms of Marxist views of the family

- the Marxist view that capitalism is unjust is rejected by many sociologists
- sociologists agree the family is influenced by economic system, however most disagree the family is shaped by its needs

Q15 Identify two criticisms of feminist views of the family

- feminists ignore the positive aspects of family life as many women enjoy running a home and bringing up children
- feminists ignore the rise of gender equality in areas of equal pay allowing women more say in decision making within the family
- there is evidence of greater gender equality within the home, with a small but increasing number of men becoming househusbands

Q16 Identify two criticisms of radical feminist views of the family

- some families are matriarchal as opposed to being patriarchal
- ignores the role of capitalism in oppressing women
- some men support the women's movement and its associated rights
- it ignores the advances made in women's rights on issues such as equal pay
- it ignores the class differences in women's position, the higher the social-class of women the greater their rights

Q17 Identify four ways in which feminist sociologists have aided our understanding of family dynamics

- the triple-shift
- the dual burden
- trouble free sex
- the emasculation of women through emotional responsibilities
- women's economic dependency on men
- patriarchal power on decision making

Q18 Identify four reasons for the for the changes in family size over the past 100 years

- geographic mobility
- influence of feminism
- dual-worker households
- child-centredness
- cost of raising children
- changes in infant mortality
- changes in social policy on welfare payments
- contraception
- changing role of women

YOUR NOTES

6 GLOSSARY

Anthropology – studying the societies and cultures, especially those of pre-industrial societies found around the globe

Bourgeoisie – a term from Marxism denoting a social-class composed of people whose livelihood comes from the ownership of capital

Capitalism – an economy based on the production of goods for sale (commodities) using waged labour; capitalists own the means of production in order to make profit.

Culture – the beliefs, values and customs of a society or social group

Ethnicity – the members of a social group who share common characteristics such as religion, language or race

Ethnography – a research method based on the detailed observation of a culture or group

Experiment/laboratory experiment –a research procedure which attempts to test a hypothesis by manipulating aspects of reality to see whether the outcome suggested by the hypothesis occurs.

Ideology – a system of ideas and beliefs which may reflect the interests of a particular social group

Institutional racism – discrimination against a particular ethnic or racial groups which is built on the processes, procedures and policies of an institution whether or not the discrimination is intended

Marketization of education - where parents have the power and choice to make a decision and "shop around" as consumers of education to see which is the best school to send their child to

Net-migration - The rate of people moving into a country less the number of people moving out of the same country

Patriarchy – a social system of male dominance based on assumptions of male superiority

Power – the capacity of individuals, groups, or social-classes to achieve goals and protect interests

Proletariat – a term from Marxism denoting a social-class of people whose livelihood comes from selling their labour in exchange for wages (see bourgeoisie)

Racism – belief that biologically rooted characteristics determine social activities and abilities as well as the inherent superiority and inferiority of different races

Self-fulfilling prophecy – happens when people act in response to behaviour which has been predicted of them which subsequently makes the prediction come true

Social class – classifications of people with broadly similar occupations, resources or styles of living

Social policy - are public services that aid the well-being of citizens

Society – the total entity formed by individuals and groups and their social relations most commonly located within a nation state

Stereotyping – where generalized qualities or attributes of a social group often prejudice the representation of that group

State – a set of institutions and system of government which exercises control over a specific geographical area and the population of that area.

Underclass – a concept used to characterize those occupying the lowest positions in society

Vocational education - educational training that provides practical experience in a particular occupational field such as learning a trade

Welfare state – the social and political institutions by which the state assumes a responsibility for the health and social welfare of its citizens

5 INDEX

ABOUT THE AUTHOR

The contents of the book have been written by sociologytwynham.com. For any other information or question you would like answering please contact us via the website. For other information on books in the series please visit the Revision page at sociologytwynham.com.